CARTOLINA
DALLA
CUCINA

Bruno Barbieri

pasta bakes
and gratins

Photography by **Riccardo Lettieri**

BIBLIOTHECA CULINARIA

Getting started

One of the most satisfying moments for any chef is the calm which descends immediately after the oven door is closed. Filled with a hearty lasagna or gratin, the work now lies with the stove while busy cooks can take time out and turn their attention to other domestic pleasures such as setting the table. Everything feels under control as the pressures of a hectic day slowly begin to unwind. It is a moment all too brief - to be savored to the fullest.

Oven-baked dishes, whether based on fresh or dried pasta, crêpes or gratins, are a cook's best friend. Substantial enough to stand alone as a main course, they can be prepared in advance and left to their own devices once in the oven.

These satisfying dishes are guaranteed crowd-pleasers. Golden brown and irresistibly crispy on top, they arrive at the table triumphant, exciting curiosity and anticipation to reveal the tender layers concealed underneath the molten cheese crust.

Pasta bakes and gratins lend themselves particularly well to adaptations: an intimate dinner for two can be transformed into a sumptuous family feast without too much fuss or complication. The same recipe can accommodate fresh seasonal foods or store cupboard ingredients depending on the season and practical considerations. A well-placed substitution (Roquefort for Gorgonzola or Swiss chard for spinach, for example) won't ruin the delicate balance of flavors: often a clever replacement can offer a new and interesting take on the original recipe.

A word of caution is necessary when experimenting with pasta bakes and gratins: the extraordinary adaptability of these dishes comes with certain drawbacks - their flexibility is not a license to improvise. Ingredients must be selected carefully, taking into consideration the compatibility of contrasting flavors, textures and cooking times. The following section offers some practical advice for achieving perfect results every time.

Balancing wet and dry ingredients. It is vital that the wet and dry ingredients complement each other to produce a moist final result: not too dry and not too runny. The water content of fresh ingredients can vary radically depending on the ripeness and cultivation methods. Take note of this during the preparation stages and make changes accordingly. For example, the added moisture of very ripe tomatoes can be compensated for by reducing other liquids in the recipe. Always keep in mind that liquid evaporates in the oven: the more time spent in the oven, the more liquid will evaporate. Similarly, dried lasagna sheets absorb more liquid than fresh lasagna sheets. Keeping the béchamel sauce (or other binding sauces) fluid is key in producing a moist result: a dry lasagna should be avoided at all costs.

Know your oven. There are a number of factors which can affect an oven's performance. Variation between brands, thermometer sensitivity, heating methods (gas or electric, with or without fan) and the age of the appliance can produce noticeably different results. Timings and temperatures are provided as guidelines: actual timings may vary depending on the efficiency of the oven. For fan-assisted ovens it may be necessary to reduce the temperature by 20°C/68°F/1 gas mark, or to shorten the cooking time. If the oven produces uneven results, try rotating the casserole dish halfway through cooking.

Fresh or dried lasagna sheets? Homemade or ready-made béchamel sauce? The answer seems straightforward. An educated palate recognizes homemade pasta: it absorbs less liquid than dried pasta and cooks more evenly. Additionally it can easily be made to fit oven dishes of any shape or size, reducing the tedious patchwork required with the one-size-fits-all dried sheets. Nevertheless, busy

modern lifestyles mean it is not always possible to prepare this quintessential Italian ingredient by hand. Making pasta from scratch requires patience and can seem a little daunting at first. Thankfully, being short on time does not mean going without lasagna. Whilst it is always preferable to use fresh pasta, dried pasta is a good alternative in situations where it is not possible to make, or get hold of, the fresh variety. Homemade béchamel sauce, on the other hand, is indispensable. Although ready-made béchamel is widely available and easy to use, the gluey texture and starchy aftertaste make it difficult to accept as a valid alternative. Homemade béchamel is surprisingly simple to prepare and much cheaper than its shop-bought counterpart. Using fresh ingredients makes a big difference to taste and texture, producing standout dishes which are well worth the extra time and effort.

Use the right oven dish. Avoid using metal dishes for pasta bakes and gratins. These dishes tend to distribute heat unevenly, causing parts of the béchamel or melted cheese to burn and give off an undesirable odor. Emile Henry dishes, manufactured in HR® (high resistance) ceramic, guarantee uniform heat distribution - perfect for controlled, natural cooking. Ideal for lasagnas, gratins and pasta bakes, they keep the contents warmer for longer once removed from the oven. The variety of sizes makes it easy to find the perfect dish for all occasions, be it a simple lasagna for one or a lavish dinner party. Available in a wide range of colors, they coordinate beautifully with any cookware collection.

Fresh pasta

Making fresh pasta may seem demanding at first, yet with a little practice it soon becomes second nature. The procedure is relatively straightforward: developing the right manual technique is key in gaining confidence. While there are no shortcuts, there are certainly a few tricks to give novices a helping hand:

- Ensure the kitchen is not over ventilated: too much air can dry out the pasta. Dry pasta is difficult to roll, tends to tear at the edges and is problematic to mold, shape and mark.
- Resting time after kneading is necessary to relax the gluten, a protein composite contained in wheat flour which renders the pasta flexible. Skipping or cutting this period short makes the pasta impossible to roll with a rolling pin and unnecessarily fiddly to use with a machine.
- Whilst oil and salt are not compulsory, they certainly help to achieve good results. The former softens the dough, making it more manageable for beginners whereas the latter enhances the flavor. If using salt, remember that it oxidizes the egg: if not used within a day the pasta will become dark in color.
- Take care not to overcook the lasagna sheets as this causes the pasta to become spongy. The pasta should remain firm to the bite, a texture known as *al dente* in Italian cuisine. The recipes reiterate the importance of plunging the lasagna sheets into cold water after boiling in order to halt the cooking process. As the pasta will undergo further cooking in the oven, this step is essential to maintain the perfect *al dente* texture.
- This step has the further advantage of removing the starch released during cooking, preventing the pasta from sticking to the dishtowel and avoiding tears at the edges.

Dried pasta

Dried lasagna sheets are widely available in supermarkets. The choice has grown substantially over the years: even the spinach version (verde) has become easy to find. Production and drying methods differ from one manufacturer to another with variable results. Consequently, when using dried pasta it is advisable to follow the cooking times specified on the packet. Remember that these products tend to absorb much more liquid than fresh pasta, so be sure to adjust the quantity of wet ingredients accordingly.

Fresh lasagna sheets **(approx. 600 g/ 21.2 oz)**

350-400 g/ 12-14 oz all-purpose flour
4 medium-sized eggs
(approx. 240 g/ 8.5 oz)

10 ml/ 2 tbsp extra virgin olive oil
1 pinch salt

Pour the flour onto a pastry board. Shape into a mound and make a well in the center. Crack the eggs into the well, add the extra virgin olive oil and a generous pinch of salt then beat with a fork. Be sure not to skip or shorten this step: the smoother the eggs, the silkier the pasta will be. Gradually work the flour into the eggs and knead for around 8 minutes until the dough is soft and elastic. Shape into a ball, cover with plastic wrap and place under a dishtowel. Leave to rest in a cool place for at least 1 hour.

Roll out the pasta with a rolling pin or machine to a thickness of around 2-3mm/0.1". Trim according to the requirements of the recipe or shape of the dish and leave to rest on a lightly floured dishtowel. Cover with another dishtowel. Keep this stage brief: leaving the lasagna sheets to rest for too long will dry the pasta out, making it crumbly and difficult to manage.

Bring plenty of salted water to the boil and cook the pasta for 2-3 minutes until *al dente*. Plunge into a bowl of cold water and leave to dry on a dishtowel.

Fresh lasagna verde sheets **(approx. 600 g/ 21.2 oz)**

250-300 g/ 8.5-10.5 oz all-purpose flour
100 g/ 3.5 oz spinach*, blanched,
squeezed dry, blended and passed
through a food mill
3 eggs (approx. 180 g/ 6.3 oz)**

10 ml/ 2 tbsp extra virgin olive oil
1 pinch salt

*May be replaced with other leafy vegetables (chard, rocket, red Treviso radicchio, nettles etc.).
**This recipe requires 1 egg less than the basic pasta to compensate for the added moisture in the spinach leaves.

Pour the flour onto a pastry board. Shape into a mound and make a well in the center. Crack the eggs into the well, add the extra virgin olive oil and a generous pinch of salt then beat with a fork until smooth. Add the spinach to the well and gradually work in the flour (if you prefer a marbled effect, finely chop the spinach instead of blending). Knead for around 8 minutes until the dough is soft and elastic. Shape into a ball, cover with plastic wrap and place under a dishtowel. Leave to rest in a cool place for at least 1 hour.

Roll out the pasta with a rolling pin or machine to a thickness of around 2-3mm/0.1". Trim according to the requirements of the recipe or shape of the dish and leave to rest on a lightly floured dishtowel. Cover with another dishtowel.

Keep this stage brief: leaving the lasagna sheets to rest for too long will dry the pasta out, making it crumbly and difficult to manage.

Bring plenty of salted water to the boil and cook the pasta for 2-3 minutes until *al dente*. Plunge into a bowl of cold water then leave to dry on a dishtowel.

Béchamel sauce

1 ltr/ 4 cups whole milk	1 pinch nutmeg*
80 g/ 2.8 oz all-purpose flour, sifted	Salt
80 g/ 2.8 oz butter	

*May be replaced with bay leaves or other herbs and spices to complement the flavors of the dish.

Pour the milk into a saucepan and bring to the boil with the salt and nutmeg. Next, melt the butter in a separate large heavy-based saucepan. Add the flour and leave to brown slightly to make a roux (the thickener which serves as the base for the béchamel sauce).

Gradually pour in the hot milk, stirring with a wooden spoon then whisking to remove any lumps. Heat over a low flame for 4-5 minutes. Pass through a fine strainer and set aside. Pay attention to the consistency, ensuring the sauce does not become too thick. For lasagna, béchamel should have a fluid yet creamy texture.

Béchamel sauce can be prepared a few hours in advance: simply cover and conserve at room temperature to prevent the sauce from thickening. If this happens, gently reheat or stir through a little hot milk.

Creamy fish sauce

250 ml/ 1 cup clam juice or fish fumet (concentrated fish stock)
150 ml/ ¾ cup fish stock
45 g/ 1.6 oz butter

45 g/ 1.6 oz flour, sifted
Salt and pepper

Melt the butter in a small heavy-based saucepan and add the flour. Cook for 4-5 minutes, stirring continuously to avoid the mixture sticking to the pan and changing color. Remove from the heat, then mix through the clam juice and fish stock. Return to the flame and bring to the boil. Season with salt and pepper, turn down the heat and cook over a gentle flame for 5 minutes.

Classic lasagna with porcini mushrooms

Traditional Italian cooking at its finest, this rustic main course has a characteristic flavor of pork meat. The irresistible richness of this dish means it can hold its own as a main course. While the original recipe calls for chicken liver, here it has been replaced by porcini mushrooms to satisfy modern palates.

Serves 4

320 g/ 11.2 oz fresh lasagna
  sheets (see p.7)
OR
175 g/ 11.2 oz dried lasagna
  sheets
500 g/ 17.6 oz lean pork
  mince, rump
200 g/ 7 oz sausage meat
250 ml/ 1 cup béchamel sauce
  (see p.8)
200 g/ 7 oz fresh porcini
  mushrooms
200 g/ 7 oz Parmesan, grated
500 ml/ 2 cups meat stock
100 g/ 3.5 oz celery,
  finely chopped
100 g/ 3.5 oz carrot, peeled
  and finely chopped
100 g/ 3.5 oz onion, peeled
  and finely chopped
2 tbsp tomato paste
1 garlic clove
Extra virgin olive oil
Few knobs butter, plus extra
  to coat the dish
Salt and pepper

First, make the Bolognese sauce. Heat a little extra virgin olive oil in a large heavy-based saucepan and sauté the vegetables. Break up the sausage meat and add to the pan along with the pork mince and tomato paste. Pour in the stock and leave to simmer over a low heat for 90 minutes. Salt and pepper to taste.

Preheat the oven to 200 °C/400 °F/gas mark 6 and coat a casserole dish with butter.

Boil the lasagna sheets in plenty of salted water for 2-3 minutes and remove with a slotted spoon. Plunge into cold water to stop the cooking process and leave to dry on a dishtowel.

Spread a thin layer of Bolognese sauce over the base of the casserole dish and cover with a single layer of lasagna sheets. Spoon over the béchamel sauce then add a layer of mushrooms. Sprinkle with grated Parmesan and repeat the process, alternating the order of ingredients and finishing with a layer of Bolognese sauce. Top with a few knobs of butter and bake in the oven for around 15 minutes. Serve drizzled with extra virgin olive oil.

Spinach lasagna verde with salmon and parsley sauce

Serves 6

640 g/ 22.5 oz fresh lasagna verde sheets (see p.7)
OR
250 g/ 22.5 oz dried lasagna verde sheets
100 g/ 3.5 oz butter

Salmon and parsley sauce

500 g/ 17.6 oz raw salmon flesh, diced
1 small onion, thinly sliced
2 slices lemon rind (unwaxed)
100 ml/ ½ cup vegetable stock or fish fumet (concentrated fish stock)
1 small bunch parsley
Extra virgin olive oil
Salt and pepper

Creamy fish sauce
(see p.9)

Preheat the oven to 180 °C/350 °F/gas mark 4 and coat a casserole dish with butter.

Heat a little extra virgin olive oil in a large non-stick frying pan and brown the onions. Add the salmon and lemon rind, cover with the vegetable stock and simmer over a low flame for approximately 10 minutes. Meanwhile, finely chop the parsley, putting a few whole leaves aside for the final garnish. Remove the salmon from the heat, season with salt and pepper and sprinkle with the chopped parsley. Drizzle with extra virgin olive oil and set aside.

Boil the lasagna sheets in plenty of salted water for 2-3 minutes and remove with a slotted spoon. Plunge into cold water to stop the cooking process and leave to dry on a dishtowel.

Spread a few tbsp of creamy fish sauce over the bottom of the casserole dish and cover with a single layer of lasagna sheets. Spoon over a layer of salmon and parsley sauce then repeat the process, alternating the order of ingredients and finishing with a layer of salmon and parsley sauce. Top with a few knobs of butter and bake in the oven for around 15 minutes until golden brown.

Bring to the table directly in the casserole dish. Alternatively, divide into individual portions and garnish with a drizzle of extra virgin olive oil and a scattering of parsley, freshly chopped just before serving.

Shredded pasta bake with creamy ham and pea sauce

This lovely vintage recipe brings back a taste of the 1970s. Popular with children and adults alike, the winning combination of cream, ham and peas gives this dish a distinct retro feel. Ideal for using leftover pasta cuttings, this dish is perfectly in keeping with the domestic waste not, want not spirit of the bygone era, fondly preserved by a generation of Italian grandmothers.

Serves 4

320 g/ 11.2 oz fresh lasagna
  sheets (see p.7)
500 ml/ 2 cups cream
200 g/ 7 oz peas, blanched
300 g/ 10.5 oz ham,
  cut into strips
150 g/ 5.3 oz Parmesan
2 egg yolks
1 small onion, finely chopped
50 g/1.8 oz butter
Salt and pepper

Preheat the oven to 200°C/400°F/gas mark 6. Butter 4 individual oven dishes or ovenproof serving plates.

Heat a knob of butter in a large heavy-based saucepan and sauté the onion. Add the ham, peas and cream, season with salt and pepper and cook over a low heat until the sauce has reduced to ¾ its original volume. Add the yolks and mix well. Cook for a few more minutes, taking care to avoid the yolks clotting.

Roll out the lasagna sheets (not too thin, approx. 3-4mm/0.2") and cut into strips. Next, cut the strips into smaller, irregular shapes, then boil in plenty of salted water until *al dente*. Remove with a slotted spoon, plunge into a bowl of cold water to stop the cooking process and leave to dry on a dishtowel.

Tip the shredded pasta into a large frying pan and toss together with the ham and pea sauce. Transfer onto the individual dishes or serving plates and sprinkle with Parmesan. Place in the oven for a few minutes until the topping forms a golden brown crust.

Mini lasagna parcels with veal and mozzarella

These stylish little parcels are perfect for creating a high-impact presentation. The shape and size can be easily adapted to cater for different requirements. Mini parcels make serving easier and guarantee a good balance of dried and fresh pasta. If opting for the elaborate full-size parcel, divide portions evenly to ensure an equal helping of both varieties.

Serves 4

4 fresh lasagna sheets:
  approx. 45 g each (see p.7)
200 ml/ ¾ cup stock
200 g/ 7 oz small pasta shapes
  such as ditalini (the smaller
  the better)
200 g/ 7 oz veal mince
100 g/ 3.5 oz pork mince
100 g/ 3.5 oz fresh lard
150 g/ 5.3 oz vegetables:
  celery, carrot and onion,
  finely chopped
100 g/ 3.5 oz Parmesan,
  grated
50 g/ 1.8 oz butter
1 mozzarella, diced
  (approx. 125 g/ 4.4 oz)
1 tbsp tomato paste
Extra virgin olive oil
Salt and pepper

Preheat the oven to 200°C/400°F/gas mark 6. Coat 4 individual oven dishes with butter.

Heat a little extra virgin olive oil in a large heavy-based saucepan and sauté the vegetables. Add the lard and continue cooking for a few minutes. Tip in the veal and pork mince along with the tomato paste then season with salt and pepper. Keep stirring until the meat changes color. Cover with the stock and leave to simmer for around 60 minutes.

Boil the lasagna in plenty of salted water for 2-3 minutes then remove with a slotted spoon. Plunge into a bowl of cold water to stop the cooking process and leave to dry on a dishtowel. Trim the lasagna sheets and line the individual baking dishes, leaving enough pasta hanging over the edges to cover the filling (approx. 15x15cm/ 6x6").

Boil the pasta shapes in plenty of salted water until *al dente*. Drain, then tip into the pan with the meat and vegetables and toss the ingredients together. Divide between the individual oven dishes, scatter over the mozzarella and sprinkle with Parmesan. Top with a few knobs of butter then close each parcel, folding the pasta back on itself to cover the filling.

Bake in the oven for around 10 minutes until golden brown.

Spiced lasagna
with four-cheese béchamel

Serves 4

340 g / 11.2 oz fresh lasagna
sheets (see p.7) flavored with:
1 pinch black pepper
1 pinch white pepper
1 pinch mace
1 pinch nutmeg

Four cheese béchamel
sauce

1 serving béchamel sauce,
  (see P.8)
100 g/ 3.5 oz sweet
Gorgonzola, diced
100 g/ 3.5 oz spicy
  Gorgonzola, diced
100 g/ 3.5 oz Taleggio cheese,
  diced (or Fontina)
100 g/ 3.5 oz Parmesan,
  grated
Salt and pepper

150 g/ 5.3 oz Parmesan,
  grated
40 g/ 1.4 oz butter

Preheat the oven to 180°C/350°F/gas mark 4 and coat a casserole dish with butter.

Prepare the lasagna sheets following the recipe on page 7, adding in the spices at the same stage as the salt.

Make up the béchamel sauce according to the recipe on page 8. Remove from the heat and gradually stir in both types of Gorgonzola along with the Taleggio and the Parmesan until the cheese has melted completely. Season with a little salt and pepper if required. The sauce should be quite fluid: if it is too thick dilute with a little hot milk.

Boil the lasagna in plenty of salted water for 2-3 minutes then remove with a slotted spoon. Plunge into a bowl of cold water to stop the cooking process and leave to dry on a dishtowel.

Spread 2 tbsp of béchamel sauce over the bottom of the casserole dish and cover with a single layer of lasagna sheets. Follow with another layer of béchamel sauce and sprinkle with Parmesan. Repeat the process, alternating the order of ingredients and finishing with a layer of béchamel sauce. Top with a few knobs of butter and bake in the oven for around 15 minutes. Transfer onto individual plates and drizzle over a little extra virgin olive oil. Serve sprinkled with spices and topped with Parmesan.

Open seafood lasagna with cherry tomatoes and thyme

A unique twist on the classic lasagna shape, "open" lasagnas make for an impressive main course. Fresh pasta is absolutely essential to complement the refined flavors and textures of this dish. Limiting the layers to three helps to keep the shape together; accordingly, the amount of pasta is less than that normally required in a lasagna for 4.

Serves 4

240 g/ 8.4 oz fresh lasagna
sheets (see p.7)
50 g/ 1.8 oz butter
to coat the dish
Fresh parsley

Tomato and shellfish sauce

1 kg/ 2.2 lb langoustines
  (also known as scampi or
  Dublin Bay prawns; 4 – 6
  per person depending
  on the size)
500 g/ 17.6 oz clams
300 g/ 10.5 oz shrimp/prawns
10 scallops
500 g/17.6 oz cherry
tomatoes, chopped
100 ml/ ½ cup fish fumet
  (concentrated fish stock)
3 garlic cloves
Fresh thyme
Dried oregano
Extra virgin olive oil
Creamy fish sauce (see p.9)

Preheat the oven to 180°C/350°F/gas mark 4 and coat the center of 4 ovenproof plates or individual oven dishes.

Prepare the langoustines and shrimp: peel off the shells, cut the langoustines into small pieces and remove the intestinal tract from the shrimps. Heat a little extra virgin olive oil in a frying pan with 2 garlic cloves and sauté the langoustines along with the shrimp and scallops for 3-4 minutes. Add the cherry tomatoes, oregano, thyme and fish fumet. Season with salt and pepper then sauté for a further 4-5 minutes.

Meanwhile, heat a little extra virgin olive oil and the remaining garlic in a separate frying pan. Add the clams, pour in a glass of water then cover and steam for 3-4 minutes until the shells open. Remove the clams from their shells and pass the cooking juices through a strainer. Tip the clams into the tomato and shellfish sauce then set aside.

Trim the pasta sheets, keeping in mind the shape of the serving plates where the open lasagna will be assembled. Cook the lasagna in plenty of boiling, salted water for 2-3 minutes then remove with a slotted spoon. Plunge into a bowl of cold water to stop the cooking process and leave to dry on a dish towel. Spoon 2 tbsp of the tomato and shellfish sauce onto each plate then arrange a single layer of lasagna sheets on top. Follow with another layer of tomato and shellfish sauce, then spoon over the creamy fish sauce. Repeat the process, alternating the order of ingredients and finishing with a layer of tomato and shellfish sauce. Bake in the oven for around 10 minutes. Drizzle over a little extra virgin olive oil, scatter with parsley and serve.

Artichoke and mint lasagna with Fontina béchamel

Serves 4

320 g/ 11.2 oz fresh lasagna
sheets (see p.7)
OR
175 g/ 11.2 oz dried lasagna
sheets
500 g/ 17.6 oz Fontina cheese,
diced
200 g/ 7 oz smoked bacon,
diced
200 g/ 7 oz Parmesan, grated
250 ml/ 1 cup béchamel sauce
(see p.8)
5 globe artichokes
1 lemon
30 g/ 1.1 oz butter
3 tbsp extra virgin olive oil
1 bay leaf
1 bunch fresh mint, finely
chopped
Dried oregano to taste
2 garlic cloves
Salt and pepper

Preheat the oven to 180°C/350°F/gas mark 4 (grill) and coat a casserole dish with butter.

Prepare the artichokes by removing the hard outer leaves and trimming away the tough fibrous part of the stalk. Scoop out and discard the furry central choke. Cut the artichoke heads into slices and dice the stalks. Immerse the artichokes in a bowl of water with a squeeze of lemon juice to prevent them from going brown. Heat a little extra virgin olive oil in a large heavy-based saucepan then add the garlic and smoked bacon together with the drained artichokes. Cook for 15 minutes until the ingredients soften to form a thick sauce. Remove from the heat, add the mint then salt and pepper to taste. Remove the garlic and set the sauce aside.

Prepare the béchamel sauce following the recipe on page 8, flavoring the milk with the bay leaf. Stir in the Fontina cheese and allow it to melt completely. Set aside.

Boil the lasagna sheets in plenty of salted water for 2-3 minutes then remove with a slotted spoon. Plunge into cold water to stop the cooking process and leave to dry on a dishtowel. Spread 2 tbsp of béchamel sauce over the bottom of the casserole dish and cover with a single layer of lasagna sheets. Spoon over the artichoke sauce then sprinkle over some Parmesan and a pinch of dried oregano. Repeat the process, alternating the order of ingredients and finishing with a layer of artichoke sauce. Sprinkle with the remaining Parmesan and bake in the oven for around 15 minutes.

Orecchiette pasta bake with sautéed king prawns and buffalo mozzarella

Orecchiette pasta shapes act as miniature bowls, cradling the perfect amount of Mediterranean sauce for a burst of intense flavor in every bite. This type of pasta is perfect for party canapés; mini ceramic dishes keep the heat in for longer and look stunning.

Serves 4

280 g/ 8.5 oz orecchiette
 pasta (may be substituted
 with other small pasta shapes
 such conchiglie or farfalle)
500 g/ 17.6 oz cherry
 tomatoes, halved
200 g/ 7 oz buffalo
 mozzarella, diced (may
 be substituted with burrata
 cheese or regular mozzarella)
20 large king prawns
5 garlic cloves, unpeeled
Fresh herbs (thyme, oregano)
Extra virgin olive oil
Butter
Salt and pepper

Preheat the oven to 180°C/350°F/gas mark 4 (grill setting) and coat a casserole dish (or a dozen mini casseroles) with butter. Heat a little extra virgin olive oil in a frying pan and sauté the prawns with the garlic. Add the cherry tomatoes and cook for few more minutes then remove the garlic.

Boil the orecchiette in plenty of salted water until *al dente*. Drain, tip into the frying pan and toss together with the prawns and tomatoes.

Pour into the casserole dish(es), top with the buffalo mozzarella and sprinkle with the fresh herbs. Place in the oven for a few minutes until the cheese has formed a golden brown crust. Remove from the oven and serve immediately.

Fusilli timbale with Bolognese sauce

This beautiful dish derives its name from the word timbale, meaning kettledrum in French. Fusilli is a good choice for those attempting their first timbale: the spiral shapes are ideal for catching the sauce and the edges slot together perfectly. Be sure to grease the dish well and remove with care in order to preserve the distinctive shape. Leaving the timbale to set briefly will make it easier to slice.

Serves 4

300 g/ 10.6 oz fusilli pasta
500 g/ 17.6 oz Bolognese
 sauce
200 g/ 7 oz peas, shelled
200 g/ 7 oz Parmesan, grated
200 g/ 7 oz Mozzarella, diced
100 g/ 3.5 oz butter
4 eggs, boiled and halved
Fresh breadcrumbs

Preheat the oven to 180°C/350°F/gas mark 4 and coat a casserole dish with butter. Sprinkle with enough breadcrumbs to coat the entire surface of the tin.

Boil the peas in salted water for a few minutes. Drain and pour into a large mixing bowl together with the Bolognese sauce.

Next, boil the fusilli in plenty of salted water until *al dente*, then drain and mix together with the Bolognese sauce and Parmesan. Leave to cool.

Arrange a few egg halves face down on the bottom of the casserole dish, tip in half of the pasta and cover with a layer of mozzarella. Add another layer of egg halves then cover with the remaining pasta.

Top with a few knobs of butter and bake in the oven for 15 minutes.

Remove from the oven and turn out onto a serving dish. Cut into slices at the dinner table.

Ziti gratin with four-cheese béchamel and escarole

This versatile recipe lends itself well to many different flavor combinations. Try potatoes, Gorgonzola and pesto for a hearty supper, or eggplant (aubergine), Parmesan and oregano for a vibrant summer dish.

Serves 6

360 g/ 11.3 oz ziti pasta (may be substituted with similar pasta shapes such as rigatoni)

1 ltr/ 4 cups milk

100 g/ 3.5 oz butter

120 g/ 4.2 oz flour

3 escarole/broadleaf endive heads (or curly endive/chicory)

100 g/ 3.5 oz Roquefort, diced (or Stilton)

120 g/ 4.2 oz Cabriolet cheese, diced (or other goat cheese)

120 g/ 4.2 oz Emmental/Swiss cheese, diced

100 g/ 3.5 oz Parmesan, grated

100 g/ 3.5 oz small Taggiasche olives, pitted (or other small black olives)

1 pinch nutmeg

2 garlic cloves

Extra virgin olive oil

Parmesan, grated

Butter to coat the dish

Preheat the oven to 200°C/400°F/gas mark 6 and coat a casserole dish with butter.

Use the milk, flour and butter to prepare the béchamel sauce according to the procedure on page 8. Season with a pinch of nutmeg.

Add the cheese using a bain-marie technique: fill a large saucepan with water and bring to a gentle simmer. Pour the béchamel sauce into a smaller saucepan or heatproof bowl then carefully lower into the large saucepan so that the simmering water surrounds the bottom of the small saucepan, gently heating the contents. Take care not to allow any water to enter the béchamel sauce. Stir in the Roquefort, Cabriolet and Emmental until they have melted completely. Keep warm.

Next, prepare the escarole. Separate the leaves then wash, dry and cut into ribbons. Heat a little olive oil in a frying pan, add the garlic and sauté the escarole. Add the olives and cook for a few more minutes.

Boil the ziti in plenty of salted water until *al dente*. Drain and add to the pan with the escarole and toss the ingredients together. Remove the garlic, then stir in the béchamel sauce, making sure the ingredients are evenly coated. Tip into the casserole dish and sprinkle with the Parmesan.

Bake in the oven for around 15 minutes until golden brown. The consistency should remain slightly fluid.

Broken spaghetti with Speck and red potatoes

Feel free to use up other types of pasta left over in the cupboards for this recipe - adjusting the cooking time accordingly to ensure uniform results. Season sparingly: the naturally intense flavor of Speck means that this dish requires very little added salt.

Serves 4

320 g/ 11.2 oz spaghetti
250 g/ 8.8 oz Speck ham, diced
3 red potatoes, peeled and diced
1 small onion, finely chopped
2 garlic cloves, unpeeled
1 chili pepper
Provolone, to taste (or Gouda)
Extra virgin olive oil
Salt and pepper

250 cl/ 10 cups vegetable stock
1 broccoli head
(approx. 500 g/ 17.6 oz)

Preheat the oven to 180°C/350°F/gas mark 4 (grill setting) and coat a casserole dish with butter.

Rinse the broccoli under cold running water, then discard the leaves and separate the florets.

Heat a little extra virgin olive oil in a heavy-based saucepan and sauté the onion, garlic and chili pepper. Add the Speck and cook until golden brown, then tip in the potatoes and cover with the stock. Season with salt and pepper and cook for 3 minutes. Add the broccoli and cook for a further 5 minutes, producing a very thin sauce with the vegetables still intact. Remove the garlic and set the sauce aside.

Break the spaghetti into small pieces and boil in plenty of salted water until *al dente*. Drain, add to the Speck and potatoes and toss the ingredients together.

Tip into the casserole dish and scatter over some grated Provolone. Place in the oven for a few minutes until golden brown.

Carbonara pasta bake with cognac and pepper

With a lower fat content than cream, stracchino produces a lighter result without sacrificing the velvety consistency characteristic of this revered dish. Season with high quality, aromatic pepper freshly ground just before serving for an unforgettable flavor.

Serves 4

280 g/ 9.8 oz penne pasta
  (rigate)
250 ml/ 1 cup milk
  (semi-skimmed)
200 g/ 7 oz stracchino
  (or other soft, creamy cheese)
150 g/ 5.3 oz pork cheeks/
  jowl bacon
100 g/ 3.5 oz pancetta
  (salted and dried)
150 g/ 5.3 oz Parmesan,
  grated
2 eggs
1 medium-sized onion, diced
70 ml/ 1/4 cup cognac
50 g/ 1.8 oz butter
Freshly ground pepper

Preheat the oven to 180°C/350°F/gas mark 4 (grill setting) and coat a casserole dish with butter.

Cut the pork cheeks and the pancetta into neat strips. Melt the butter in a large heavy-based saucepan and sauté the onion. Add the pork cheeks and pancetta strips, pour in the cognac and leave to evaporate for 2 minutes.

Blend the milk, stracchino and eggs together in a food processor then set aside.

Boil the penne in plenty of salted water until *al dente*. Drain, tip into the saucepan with the pork cheeks and pancetta and toss the ingredients together. Leave to cool then stir in the blended stracchino.

Transfer the pasta to the casserole dish, sprinkle with Parmesan and top with a few knobs of butter. Place in the oven for a couple of minutes until golden brown.

Remove from the oven, season with plenty of freshly ground pepper and serve.

Gramigna pasta bake with sausage meatballs

For a vegetarian version, try substituting the meat with potatoes together with Swiss chard or eggplant (aubergine), lightly flavored with a little garlic.

Serves 4

280 g/ 8.5 oz gramigna pasta
  (may be substituted with
  similar pasta shapes,
  such as macaroni)
400 g/ 14.1 oz sausage meat
250 ml/ 1 cup cream
2 eggs
1 slice homemade bread,
  soaked in a little milk
1 small onion, thinly sliced
1 small bunch basil
Medium-aged Pecorino,
  to taste
Extra virgin olive oil
Butter
Salt and pepper

Preheat the oven to 180°C/350°F/gas mark 4 (grill setting) and coat a casserole dish with butter.

Place the sausage meat in a mixing bowl along with the eggs and crumbled bread. Mix well, then season with salt and pepper. Divide the mixture into small pieces and roll into mini meatballs.

Heat a little extra virgin olive oil in a heavy-bottomed saucepan and sauté the onion. Tip in the mini meatballs and cook for 7-8 minutes. Add the cream along with the basil leaves and cook for a further 3-4 minutes.

Boil the gramigna in plenty of salted water and cook until *al dente*. Drain, tip into the meatball sauce and toss the ingredients together.

Pour the pasta into the casserole dish and scatter over some grated Pecorino.

Place in the oven for around 4-5 minutes until the cheese turns golden brown. Bring to the table directly in the casserole dish or divide between individual serving plates, drizzled with extra virgin olive oil.

Sedanini pasta bake with chicken, eggplant and mozzarella

Let fresh seasonal produce dictate the flavors in this recipe. The delicate composition of ingredients should be balanced according to personal taste - working together like notes in a musical harmony. Try experimenting with zucchini, lamb and curry or tomatoes, pork cheeks and chili pepper.

Serves 4

280 g/ 8.5 oz sedanini pasta (may be substituted with similar tubular pasta shapes such as penne)
300 g/ 10.6 oz chicken sausages, finely chopped
2 eggplants/aubergines (approx. 600 g/ 1.3 lb)
2 buffalo mozzarella, diced (approx. 260 g/ 9.1 oz; may be replaced with regular mozzarella)
Fresh herbs (thyme, oregano)
3 garlic cloves
Parmesan, to taste
1 small bunch parsley
Extra virgin olive oil
Butter
Coarse sea salt

Preheat the oven to 200°C/400°F/gas mark 6 and coat a casserole dish with butter.

Peel the eggplants with a potato peeler and cut into large cubes. Tip into a colander, sprinkle over some salt and leave for 30 minutes to draw out the excess moisture.

Rinse under cold water and dry on a piece of kitchen towel. Heat a little extra virgin olive oil in a large frying pan and add the garlic. Tip in the eggplant and sauté for 3-4 minutes.

Next, place the chicken and the mozzarella in a separate colander to drain the juices. Wash, dry and finely chop the parsley.

Boil the sedanini in plenty of salted water until *al dente* then drain and add to the eggplant. Tip in the sausage and mozzarella along with the fresh herbs and toss the ingredients together, making sure they are evenly coated. Remove the garlic.

Pour into the casserole dish and sprinkle with some grated Parmesan. Scatter over the parsley and transfer to the oven for a couple of minutes. Once the cheese has formed a golden brown crust, remove from the oven and serve immediately.

Rigatoni stuffed with smoked turkey, nuts and red Treviso radicchio

This dish boasts an exquisite fusion of pasta with delicately smoky undertones - an unconventional combination in Italian cuisine. The key lies in keeping the smoky aroma subtle. Be sure to choose a good quality, lightly aromatic smoked turkey or duck.

Serves 6

36 rigatoni pasta shapes
(large enough to stuff)
250 g/ 8.8 oz smoked turkey,
finely chopped
200 g/ 7 oz nuts, finely
chopped (hazelnuts, pine
nuts and pistachios)
100 g/ 3.5 oz sheep ricotta
(or standard ricotta)
1 red Treviso radicchio head
(or endive)
150 g/ 5.3 oz Parmesan,
grated
30 g/ 1.1 oz aged Pecorino
cheese (or ricotta salata)
2 egg yolks
Butter
Extra virgin olive oil
Salt and pepper

Preheat the oven to 180°C/350°F/gas mark 4 and coat a casserole dish with butter.

Cook the rigatoni until *al dente*, plunge into cold water to stop the cooking process then drain.

Next, prepare the filling. Place the turkey, ricotta and nuts in a mixing bowl, add the Parmesan and stir in the egg yolks. Mix well, then season with salt and pepper. Spoon into in a pastry bag and set aside.

Wash and dry the radicchio. Cut into small pieces, drizzle over a little extra virgin olive oil and sprinkle with salt and pepper.

Using the pastry bag, fill the rigatoni one by one. Take care not to over-stuff: the filling expands during cooking and may cause the rigatoni to split. Arrange into neat rows along the base of the casserole dish. Scatter over the radicchio, sprinkle with the Pecorino and transfer to the oven for a few minutes until the cheese has formed a golden brown crust.

Serve with a drizzle of extra virgin olive oil.

Gnocchi gratin with asparagus

Serves 4

Gnocchi

500 g/ 17.6 oz red potatoes
125 g/ 4.4 oz flour
70 g/ 2.5 oz butter, melted
70 g/ 2.5 oz Parmesan, grated
1 whole egg
1 egg yolk
1 bunch asparagus
  (white or green)

Gorgonzola sauce

240 ml/ 1 cup milk
200 g/ 7 oz sweet Gorgonzola,
diced (or regular Gorgonzola)
50 g/ 1.8 oz mascarpone
40 g/ 1.4 oz walnuts, finely
chopped
40 g/ 1.4 oz almonds, sliced
40 g/ 1.4 oz pistachios, finely
chopped

40 g/1.4 oz butter
  to coat the dish
50 g/ 1.8 oz Parmesan, grated

Gnocchi

Preheat the oven to 170 °C/325°F/gas mark 3 (grill setting) and coat a casserole dish with butter.

Wash the potatoes and pat dry. Wrap in baking foil and transfer to the oven for approximately 1 hour until tender. Peel the potatoes, pass through a potato mill (or mash until smooth) then transfer onto a pastry board. Once cooled, put in a large mixing bowl together with the flour and the melted butter. Stir in the egg and the egg yolk then add the Parmesan. Bring the dough together and knead for a few minutes. Cover and set aside for 30 minutes. Next, divide the dough into 4 equal parts. Using the palm of your hand, roll each part into a long rope shape and cut into small even-sized pieces. Make ridges using a fork. Transfer onto a lightly floured plate and keep in the fridge until required.

Asparagus

Prepare the asparagus, discarding the tough ends and rinsing under cold water to remove any debris. Cut into small pieces and boil in plenty of salted water for a few minutes. Drain, leave to cool and set aside.

Gorgonzola sauce

Make a bain-marie: fill a small saucepan with milk then heat gently by lowering into a larger saucepan filled with simmering water. Stir in the Gorgonzola and mascarpone until completely melted.

Gratin

Place the asparagus in a large mixing bowl and pour over the Gorgonzola. Mix well. Bring plenty of salted water to the boil, add the gnocchi and remove with a slotted spoon a few seconds after they have risen to the surface. Tip into a bowl with the asparagus and toss the ingredients together. Pour into the casserole dish and sprinkle with the mixed nuts and Parmesan. Transfer to the oven for approximately 5-6 minutes until golden brown.

Tomino and Speck crêpes with tomato and basil

Serves **4**

Crêpe batter

250 ml/ 1 cup milk
100 g/ 3.5 oz all-purpose flour
2 eggs, beaten
Salt and pepper

Speck and tomino filling

12 slices Speck ham
4 red tomatoes (firm)
4 tomino cheese rounds
 (or goat cheese)
1 small Tropea red onion,
 sliced (or regular red onion)
70 g/ 2.4 oz Parmesan, grated
4-5 leaves basil
Extra virgin olive oil

Preheat the oven to 180°C/350°F/gas mark 4 (grill setting) and coat four individual-sized oven dishes with oil.

Sift the flour into a mixing bowl, add a pinch of salt and pour in the milk. Blend with an immersion blender until velvety smooth with no lumps. Add the eggs and mix thoroughly. Pass the mixture through a sieve, cover and put in the fridge for approximately 30 minutes.

Heat a non-stick frying pan and pour a small ladleful of the crêpe mixture into the center. Tip the pan from side to side, evenly coating the base with the batter. Cook for one minute, shaking the pan from time to time to prevent the mixture from sticking. Once golden brown, flip the pancake, cook the other side and set aside. Repeat this process until no batter remains (you should obtain 10-12 crêpes). Leave to cool.

Meanwhile, prepare the tomatoes. Slice off the top, remove the skins and cut into slices. Set aside.

Heat a little extra virgin olive oil in a frying pan and sauté the onion.

Place the crêpes on a pastry board and lay over a slice of Speck. Arrange a few slices of tomato and onion on top and sprinkle with Parmesan. Roll up the crêpes and cut into pieces approximately 5-6 cm/2" wide.

Place one tomino round in each oven dish, top with a few crêpe slices and transfer to the oven for 2 minutes until the cheese has melted. Drizzle with olive oil and garnish with a fresh basil leaf.

Pumpkin and mushroom roll

Serves **4-6**

Crêpe

250 g/ 8.8 oz all-purpose flour
4 eggs, beaten
1 egg yolk, beaten
500ml/ 2 cups milk
1 knob butter, melted
Salt and white pepper

Pumpkin and mushroom filling

500 g/ 17.6 oz pumpkin flesh
4 large porcini mushrooms
70 g/ 2.5 oz dried mushrooms
2 garlic cloves
Parsley
Extra virgin olive oil
Parmesan, grated
Salt and pepper

Butter to coat the dish

Crêpe

Preheat the oven to 180°C/350°F/gas mark 4 and grease a shallow oven tray (11 x 19 cm/ 4 X 17.5") with butter spray or a thin coating of butter. Mix the flour, beaten eggs and egg yolk together in a large bowl. Add the butter and blend evenly. Season with salt and pepper and pass through a strainer. Pour the mixture into the oven tray, evenly coating the base. Bake in the oven for 4-5 minutes. Turn out onto a piece of greaseproof paper and leave to cool.

Pumpkin and mushroom filling

Remove any debris from the fresh mushrooms using a soft brush and a damp dishcloth. Slice, heat a little olive oil in a frying pan and sauté the mushrooms, garlic and finely chopped parsley with a pinch of salt and pepper. Soak the dried mushrooms in warm water. Drain, squeeze out any excess moisture and add to the fresh mushrooms. Bake the pumpkin in the oven for 30 minutes until soft. Remove from the oven and pass through a food mill to make a puree.

Assemble the roll

Carefully spread the pumpkin stuffing over the crêpe, cover with a layer of mushrooms and scatter over some Parmesan. Gently roll up the crêpe to form a tube. Cut into thick slices. Coat an oven dish with butter, arrange the slices then top with a few knobs of butter and a sprinkling of Parmesan. Place under the grill for a couple of minutes until golden brown. Serve drizzled with extra virgin olive oil.

Endive gratin
with orange marinated chicken strips

The ever-appealing coupling of poultry and fruit produces original and interesting gratins. Other appetiz-ing combinations include duck and figs, guinea-fowl and plums or quail and cherry. If using dried fruit, soak in a little warm water or brandy before cooking.

Serves 4

600 g/1.3 lb chicken breast
3 endive heads
2 oranges
200 g/ 7 oz Gruyere cheese, grated
100 g/3.5 oz Parmesan, grated
3 garlic cloves, peeled
1 sprig rosemary
140 ml/ ½ cup extra virgin olive oil
Salt and pepper

Preheat the oven to 180°C/350°F/gas mark 4 (grill setting) and coat a casserole dish with butter.

Slice off the top and bottom of the orange with a sharp knife. Remove the peel: place a bowl underneath to collect the juices then cut around the edge of the orange, taking care to remove all of the white pith. Separate the segments. Make an incision along the inner part of each segment and peel away their outer skins. Cut into large chunks and set aside.

Slice the chicken into thin strips and leave to marinate in a small bowl together with the extra virgin olive oil and orange juice. Add the garlic cloves and rosemary and transfer to the fridge for a few hours. Remove the chicken from the marinate and sear in a frying pan over a high heat for a few minutes. Add the orange and cook for a further 2 minutes. Set aside.

Next, prepare the endive. Discard the core and the tough outer leaves, rinse under running water and blot dry. Cut into thin strips, drizzle over a little extra virgin olive oil and season with salt and pepper.

Arrange the endive along the bottom of the casserole dish then add the chicken together with the orange. Sprinkle with the Gruyere and Par-mesan, drizzle over a little extra virgin olive oil and season with salt and pepper. Place in the oven for a few minutes until the cheese melts and turns golden brown. Serve directly from the casserole dish.

Seared chicken gratin with leek and goat cheese sauce

The toasted baguette takes on a lovely crouton-like quality in this recipe. Feel free to experiment with other types of bread to absorb the succulent cooking juices.

Serves 4

2 leeks
400 g/ 14.1 oz chicken sausages (approx. 4 per person)
4 goat cheese rounds
150 ml/ ¾ cup cream
1 baguette
2 garlic cloves
1 sprig rosemary
1 tbsp chives, finely chopped, plus a few stems for the garnish
Extra virgin olive oil
Butter
Salt and pepper
Coarse sea salt

Preheat the oven to 180°C/350°F/gas mark 4 (grill setting) and coat a casserole dish with butter.

Carefully wash the leeks then remove the roots and the dark green part of the leaves. Slice into medium-thick rounds and rinse under cold water to remove any debris. Pour a little extra virgin olive oil in a frying pan and sauté the leek for 2 minutes. Season with salt and pepper then set aside.

Cut the baguette into slices approximately 3 cm/1.2" thick and toast in a frying pan with a drizzle of olive oil and a sprinkling of coarse sea salt.

Melt the goat cheese using a bain-marie technique: fill a large saucepan with water then bring to a gentle simmer. Tip the goat cheese into a smaller saucepan or heatproof bowl. Carefully lower into the large pan so that the simmering water surrounds the bottom of the small pan, gently heating the contents. Take care not to allow any surrounding water to enter the goat cheese. Stir until the goat cheese has melted into a thick cream. Add the chives.

Heat a separate frying pan over a high flame. Sear the chicken sausages for a few minutes together with the garlic and rosemary. Cover and keep warm.

Line the bottom of the casserole dish with the toasted baguette, then add the leek and top with the chicken sausages. Finally, pour over the melted goat cheese and place in the oven for a couple of minutes until golden brown. Serve drizzled with extra virgin olive oil.

Bell peppers stuffed with prosciutto and Fontina cheese

These peppers are just the thing for those with a penchant for distinctive flavors. Look for plump peppers which will keep their shape during cooking. Ideal for the barbeque, the charcoal grill lends a light, smoky aroma perfectly befitting of the flavors in this recipe.

Serves 4

4 bell peppers (red, yellow, orange and green)
10 small slices prosciutto
10 thin slices Fontina cheese
4 slices lightly smoked salmon, diced (preferably marinated in extra virgin olive oil, salt and pepper)
3 anchovies, finely chopped
1 slice homemade bread, toasted and finely chopped
Butter

Preheat the oven to 180°C/350°F/gas mark 4 (grill setting) and coat a casserole dish with oil.

Wash the peppers and quarter them lengthwise. Scoop out the core together with the seeds and trim away the internal white fibers.

Next, prepare the stuffing. Place the bread, anchovies and salmon together in a bowl and mix well.

Spoon the stuffing into the peppers, arrange in neat rows along the base of the casserole dish and transfer to the oven for 10 minutes. Remove from the oven, top with slices of prosciutto and Fontina cheese then place under the grill for a further 2 minutes until the cheese has melted.

Delicious served hot or at room temperature.

Cauliflower gratin with anchovies

Umami, the elusive fifth taste, is prominent in both the Parmesan and anchovies in this recipe. Despite the Japanese origin of the name, umami features in the cuisine of many different cultures. If anchovies don't appeal, try adding salted fish roe or finely chopped Bresaola (mature, salted Italian beef) to preserve the tantalizing umami flavor.

Serves 6

2 cauliflower heads (medium-large, approx. kg 1,2/ 2.7 lb each)
100 g/ 3.5 oz fresh breadcrumbs
100 g/ 3.5 oz sweet Gorgonzola, diced (or regular Gorgonzola)
50 g/ 1.8 oz Parmesan, grated
10 anchovy fillets, finely chopped
2 tbsp parsley, finely chopped
20 cl/ ¾ cup white wine vinegar
Extra virgin olive oil
Butter
Salt and pepper

Preheat the oven to 180°C/350°F/gas mark 4 (grill setting) and coat a casserole dish with butter.

Prepare the cauliflower by discarding the leaves and trimming the stalk. Bring plenty of salted water to the boil and pour in a little white wine vinegar. Tip in the cauliflower and cook until *al dente*. Drain, divide into florets and leave to cool.

Meanwhile, mix the breadcrumbs, Parmesan and parsley together in a small bowl. Season with salt and pepper.

Place the cauliflower in the casserole dish and sprinkle with the breadcrumbs. Scatter over the anchovies, top with Gorgonzola and drizzle with extra virgin olive oil.

Transfer to the oven. Once the Gorgonzola has melted, turn up the heat and cook until golden brown.

Mussel gratin with Provola cheese and pancotto bread soup

This recipe offers a lighter twist on a classic southern Italian dish. For a more filling version, add in the traditional potatoes and tomatoes and substitute the orange peel with a little oregano.

Serves 4

2 kg/ 4.4 lb mussels
 (with shells)
300 g/ 10.6 oz Provola dolce,
 diced (or Gouda)
100 g/ 3.5 oz fresh
 breadcrumbs
1 bunch parsley,
 finely chopped
2 garlic cloves
1 sprig rosemary
A few sprigs thyme
½ orange rind, grated
 (unwaxed)
Extra virgin olive oil
Salt and pepper

Preheat the oven to 180°C/350°F/gas mark 4 (grill setting) and coat a casserole dish with butter.

Immerse the mussels in a large bowl of salted water and leave to soak for a few minutes. Prepare them one at a time: discard the beard (the fibers which protrude from the shells) and scrub the shells with a knife or wire wool to remove any debris. Rinse thoroughly in salted water.

Heat a little extra virgin olive oil in a large frying pan and tip in the mussels. Cover and steam the mussels over a medium flame for a few minutes until they open. Remove the shells (discarding any unopened) and drizzle over a little extra virgin olive oil. Add the garlic clove and sprinkle with the parsley and orange rind.

Toast the breadcrumbs in a separate pan along with the remaining garlic, rosemary and thyme. Season with salt and pepper.

Arrange the mussels along the bottom of the casserole dish then sprinkle with the Provola and breadcrumbs.

Heat in the oven for a few minutes until the cheese has melted.

Divide onto individual serving plates directly at the table. Serve accompanied by fresh mixed salad leaves, garnished with extra virgin olive oil and good quality red wine vinegar.

Monkfish and bell pepper gratin with zucchini and herbs

Serves 4

800g/1.8 lb monkfish
(without head)
3 zucchinis/courgettes, peeled
1 bell pepper
50 g/ 1.8 oz fresh
  breadcrumbs
50 g/ 1.8 oz Parmesan, grated
2 garlic cloves
2 tbsp parsley, finely chopped
2 tbsp chives, finely chopped
1 sprig thyme
1 sprig rosemary
Extra virgin olive oil
Salt and pepper

Preheat the oven to 180°C/350°F/gas mark 4 (grill setting) and coat a casserole dish with oil.

Cut the zucchinis into rounds and sauté in a frying pan together with a garlic clove. Season with salt and pepper then set aside.

Wash the pepper and cut in half lengthwise. Remove the stem, scoop out the core along with the seeds and trim away the internal white fibers. Slice into neat strips.

Pour a little olive oil in a frying pan then add the remaining garlic clove and thyme. Add the pepper, sauté for 2 minutes and set aside.

Toast the breadcrumbs in a non-stick pan together with the chives and parsley for 2 minutes. Put to one side.

Wash the monkfish and cut away the skin with a sharp knife. Remove the fins with kitchen scissors and thinly slice the remaining flesh. Heat a little extra virgin olive oil in a frying pan, add the rosemary and fry on both sides for 2 minutes until golden brown.

Arrange the zucchini slices along the bottom of the casserole dish then sprinkle with the breadcrumbs and Parmesan. Add a layer of peppers and top with the monkfish. Drizzle with a little extra virgin olive oil and transfer to the oven until golden brown.

Divide onto individual plates, garnish with freshly chopped parsley and serve.

Sweet pineapple lasagna

In the depths of winter when low temperatures call for a comforting final course, fruit gratins provide a welcome solution to the "last minute dessert" dilemma. Seasonal offerings - fresh apples and pears - are well-known favorites, but don't be afraid to experiment with more unconventional flavors such as tropical fruit or fruit in syrup.

Serves 4

1 pineapple, (ripe)
250 g/ 8.8 oz walnuts
150 g/ 5.3 oz brown sugar
50 g/ 1.8 oz butter
1 bunch fresh mint

Spiced syrup

430 ml/ 1 ¾ cups water
175 g/ 6.2 oz granulated sugar
2-3 star anise
1 tbsp cardamom
1 tbsp cloves
1 licorice root

First, prepare the syrup. Heat a heavy-bottomed saucepan over a medium flame then gradually dissolve the sugar in the water. Stir continuously, taking care not to let the water boil. Once the temperature has reached 125°C/257°F, remove from the heat. Tie the spices together in a small gauze, add to the syrup and leave to infuse for 24 hours.

Preheat the oven to 180°C/350°F/gas mark 4 (grill setting).

Slice off the top and bottom of the pineapple, remove the peel and cut into very thin slices, preferably with a mandorline or slicer.

Remove the spices from the syrup, add the pineapple slices and leave to soak for 2 hours at room temperature.

Arrange the pineapple slices across the base of the casserole dish, add a layer of walnuts and sprinkle with the brown sugar and a few mint leaves. Add more layers, alternating the order of ingredients and finishing with a sprinkling of brown sugar.

Place in the oven for a few minutes until the sugar has caramelized.

Bring to the table directly in the casserole dish or transfer onto individual serving plates. Serve with red fruit ice cream or lime sorbet garnished with fresh mint.

Marinated peach gratin with almond crumble and mint

A deliciously simple dish, this gratin is equally appealing with apricots in syrup. Adding a handful of crushed amaretto biscuits to the crumble accentuates the almond flavor. The novel contrast between the crumbly topping and velvety smooth peaches makes for a wonderfully rich texture.

Serves 4

8 peaches in syrup
200 g/ 7 oz cornmeal/maize flour
200 g/ 7 oz all-purpose flour
200 g/ 7 oz almonds, shelled and finely chopped
200 g/ 7 oz granulated sugar
150 g/ 5.3 oz butter, melted
2 egg yolks
20 ml/ 1 tablespoon grappa or cognac
1 bunch fresh mint

Preheat the oven to 150°C/300°F/gas mark 2 and coat a casserole dish with butter.

Chop the peaches into small-medium sized chunks. Sprinkle with the granulated sugar and mint and leave to marinate for approximately 30 minutes.

Meanwhile, make the crumble. Place the cornmeal, flour and almonds together in a mixing bowl then stir in the egg yolks and melted butter. Mix thoroughly, pour in the grappa and stir once more.

Cover the bottom of the casserole dish with half of the crumble, arrange a layer of peaches on top and pour over the marinating juices. Sprinkle with the remaining crumble.

Bake in the oven for 45 minutes until golden brown. Serve with an iced-peach and lemon smoothie.

Caramelized pear gratin with Pecorino cheese

An intriguing union between the cheese course and the dessert, this recipe brings together the ever-appealing combination of pears and cheese. The nut brittle completes the dish, offsetting the soft textures with a delectable crunch and adding an exquisite hint of caramel.

Serves 4

4 William pears
150 g/ 5.3 oz medium-aged
  Pecorino, grated
500 ml/ 2 cups Lambrusco
  or similar semisweet red wine
2 tbsp granulated sugar
Butter

Syrup
450 ml/ 1¾ cups water
200 g/ 7 oz granulated sugar
3-4 star anise
1 cinnamon stick
100 g/ 3.5 oz nut brittle
  (preferably hazelnut)

Preheat the oven to 180°C/350°F/gas mark 4 (grill setting) and coat a casserole dish with butter. Prepare the syrup: place a heavy-bottomed saucepan over a medium flame and gradually dissolve the sugar in the water. Continue stirring, taking care not to let the water boil. Tie the spices together in a small piece of gauze, add to the pan and heat the syrup to 125°C/ 257°F.

Peel the pears and immerse them into the syrup whole. Cook for approximately 5 minutes and leave to cool in the syrup to intensify the flavor. Slice the pears lengthwise, discarding the core and the stalk. Lay the slices across the bottom of the casserole dish.

Bring the Lambrusco to the boil and reduce until it takes on a syrup-like consistency. Pour over the pairs, sprinkle with the Pecorino and place in the oven for 2 minutes until golden brown.

Garnish with the crushed hazelnut brittle.

Index